Moods
Of
Life

Moods Of Life

A Collection of Christian Poetry
centering around Real Life Issues.

Charles M. West

Pittsburgh, PA

ISBN 1-56315-117-0

Poetry/Inspirational
© Copyright 1999 Charles M. West
All rights reserved
First Printing—1999
Library of Congress #98-88434

Request for information should be addressed to:

> SterlingHouse Publisher, Inc.
> The Sterling Building
> 440 Friday Road
> Department T-101
> Pittsburgh, PA 15209

Cover design & typesetting: Drawing Board Studios

All rights reserved. No part of this publication may be reproduced, stored in a retrieval system, or transmitted in any form or by any means—electronic, mechanical, photocopy, recording or any other, except for brief quotations in printed reviews—without prior permission of the publisher.

"Scripture taken from the HOLY BIBLE INTERNATIONAL VERSION. Copyright (1973, 1978, 1984) International Bible Society. Used by permission of Zondervan Bible Publishers."

Grateful acknowledgement is made to my business partner and best friend: Dexter G. Dabney.

Other acknowledgements: My parents Michael and Sandra Johnson: I love you with all my heart and soul, thank you both for always being there for me and without your undying love and patience this would not have been possible, Dr. Tony Evans: You are truly a blessing within my life!, Pastor Martin Hawkins: Thank you for always guiding me into the light., A. J. "Clicks" Jones, Jeff Coleman, Glenn Fox, and David Waldon, Michael and Sandra Carter, Rev. Andre' Sims, Rev. Sling Patterson, Rev. David Sims, Rev. Gerard Davis, Rev. Henry Mass, Robert Toney, Sr., Sonja Jackson, Terri Williams, Deborah White, All the local radio stations & newspapers.

Printed in Canada

Dedicated to the Father,
Jesus Christ,
Whom I owe my life to.
All that I do,
is for Your glory!

Table of Contents

Foreword ix
Introduction xi

Chapter 1
God, Family, & Life 1

A Silent Cry 3
A Right That's Mine 3
Enough 4

My Savior Is He 5
Never Too Old 6
Mother, I Need 7
A Blessing 8
Hear His Words 9
Labeled A Failure 10
Standing Firm 11
Case Closed 12
On My Knees 13
Sing Out Loud 14
Trust In Me 15
The Visit 16

Give Me A Man's Love 18
All Is Well With Jesus 18
I Didn't Want You To Go 19
Natural High 19
No Longer 20
See You Soon 20
Open Your Eyes 21
Gotta Go 21

Special Introduction to Chapter Two
23

Chapter Two
Motivation & Inspiration 25

Work Of Art 26
Keep Your Dreams Alive 26
Stay With Me 27
Corruption 27
A Summer's Breeze 28
Crossing The Line 28
It's Gonna Be Alright 28
Trust In God 29
Keep Believing 29
Where Are We Bound 29
Wisdom For Today #1 30
Wisdom For Today #2 30
Give Thanks 30
Pulling Together 31
On Top 31
The Road Ahead 32
A New Beginning 32
Let Jesus Be The Boss 33
Riches Of The World 33

A Smile For You 34
The More I 34
Our Candles Burn 35
Thoughts Of Spring 35
Teach Me More 35
Guide Them All The Way 36
By The Grace Of God 36
Trust 37
What's Going On…? 37
Tick Tock 38
Make It Multiply 38
Remember 39
In All Things 39
Strong In Faith 39
Saying Good-bye 40
Each Day 40
One Day 41

Chapter Three **43**
Friends and Friendships

Thinking Of You 44	A Love Not Known 47
A Lifetime Friendship 44	Peace At Mind 47
Happy Birthday 45	Much Respect 47
Come To Me 45	Forever…Your Friend 48
Thanks 45	Give Him You 48
My Friend 46	A Thought For You 48
Friend For Life 46	A Hold On Emotions 49

Closing Remarks From The Author 51
More Acknowledgements 52

Foreword

Charles West represents a growing cadre of African American writers and authors who are able to effectively communicate to the heart and the head without compromising either. As his pastor since he was a child, I have had the privilege of seeing Charles grow and develop from a young impetuous little boy into the dynamic, effervescent young man that he has become today. I must admit however that this unique talent of composing his thoughts, reflections, and passions into poetic masterpieces stayed hidden from me until recently. As I began to interact with Charles on the many love sonnets he began crafting in honor of his wife, and as I began hearing him recite them for others, it did not take long for me to realize that I was watching a miracle in the making.

This masterful book of poetry not only is entitled *Moods of Life* but it also allows the reader to experience those "moods" for his or herself. Communicated with clarity, precision and excellence, this work will not only reflect back to you the moods you are currently experiencing as you read each piece, it will also change your mood into that which is uniquely a part of each poetic presentation. But that's not all. *Moods of Life* also is chock full of content. It is not merely empty reflections for empty heads designed to manipulate your emotions. It reflects the world view of a man who takes God, family, friends and life very seriously.

The uniqueness of this work is that it will force the readers to assess their own world view in light of the alternative one offered by Mr. West. After you have digested this work, many of your former presuppositions will be challenged and perhaps even undermined as Charles' words dig deep inside your **SOUL**. Believe me they are written as such as *to not* let your *soul* loose until the *reader has taken* seriously the implications of a Christian world view as it relates to the things that matter most.

It is one thing to read a book, it's quite another to read a man. In reading this book you will also get to know a person. A person that I have come to love, respect, and admire. A man who takes seriously his faith, his family and his future. A man who is not satisfied to merely reflect on how things are but who really is coming to know and experience how things ought to be.

Therefore it is with a great deal of confidence and conviction that I commend to you *Moods of Life*. I am confident that you will find it enjoyable, challenging and thoughtful. I am convinced that you will be convinced to reassess your own values in light of the thoughts behind the words. And when the last poem has been read and the book has been closed, something special will have happened with the moods of your own life.

Dr. Tony Evans
Senior Paster
Bible Fellowship

Introduction

I have come to learn one thing and that is if you put your trust in God, anything is possible and nothing is unreachable. I never imagined that I would be writing poetry, yet alone books. I was more into writing lyrics for songs which technically makes poetry the foundation.

As time went on, I began to focus more on my poetry. I began to write about reality. See, reality is very important when I write. I write with a purpose and that purpose is to touch someone's heart. We must come to grip that not everyone will be able to be touched by the same thing or same person or same way. So, we must use our gifts, not just in our homes, but out in the world. If we are going to make a difference in the world, then we must do it the way God wants us to and that is by being faithful to Him always.

My purpose for writing *Moods Of Life* is to let people know that it is okay to voice your thoughts and feelings. As Christians, we need to get out and do God's work and that is spreading His love all around. We must remember that we are here for others and not ourselves. Also, you can't do this by sitting at home all the time. Truth is reality. God has given me this wonderful talent and I want to share it with the world.

I write not because I have to, but because I feel that it is God's will. Through my writings, I pray that someone will be touched and decide to turn their life around and live for Jesus.

We must remember that there is no love greater than the love of God, so let's spread His love! I pray that my book will touch and motivate you. God bless you!

Charles M. West

Chapter One
God, Family, & Life

"The Lord is my shepherd, I shall not want. He makes me lie down in green pastures, He leads me beside quiet waters, He restores my soul. He guides me in the paths of righteousness for His name's sake. Even though I walk through the valley of the shadow of death, I will fear no evil, for you are within me; your rod and your staff, they comfort me. You prepare a table before me in the presence of my enemies. You anoint my head with oil; my cup overflows. Surely goodness and love will follow me all the days of my life, and I will dwell in the house of the Lord forever."—Psalm 23

Even though there is so much happening in the world today, we must still focus on God. No matter how tough times may become, God will never forsake us. You need to have complete faith and watch God perform His miracles. Remember, we all face some kind of obstacle within our lives. No one is perfect. Some of us are just able to bounce back quicker than others.

Now, this section is mainly focused on the realities of the title, "God, Family & Life." Meaning, you will read about praise, sorrow, pain, and neglect. I could not ignore these life-like situations, like some books tend to do. We must be honest with ourselves and acknowledge the wrong, for this is the only way that we can make it right. In this section, as I said earlier, I speak about abuse and you might ask why. Well, I've known several women who were in abusive relationships and to be honest with you, before it all started, these women used to be very outgoing and very out spoken.

Months soon came to pass and the marks on their bodies, for a longer period, started to last. They were becoming more and more afraid, but they felt like it was none of my business. Well, to make a long story short, 3 out of 7 of the ladies died. And the remaining four were raped. Now, if we spoke more about abuse, then I'm sure it would bring more ladies out of those kind of relationships before they too are raped or even killed.

Also, I speak about neglect within this section. We as parents, husbands, and wives sometimes get so caught up in the world, that we forget about what is most important, our families. And making sure that God is in their lives as well as our own. If there is no attention given, then we are headed for a dead end. We must learn to have more patience and be more understanding. We must stop being so judgmental. We must stop envying one another. We must open up our hearts completely to the Lord in order to make a change. If not, then the worries of the world will still block our sight from the Lord.

See, if God can die on the cross at Calvary, to save a wretch like me, then I must go out and be a witness for the Lord. I want to feel His love multiply all across the world. The way that I feel about the Lord really cannot be put into words, all I can say is, "Uhn! Uhn! Uhn!" I am very sure that there are many more people out there that feel the same way I feel about the Lord. Now, I know that my way of spreading God's word is different and is not traditional, but what we must remember is that we are not living in traditional times anymore. My brothers and sisters, it is time that we wake up and spread the good news about Jesus Christ. The world is changing and it doesn't look like it is for the better. We as Christians have a lot of work to do and it is time that we all stand up.

What good is it to be saved and only worry about one's own self? This will not make the world a better place. This will only give satisfaction to Satan because we are not bringing others to know Christ. This leaves more lost souls for Satan to conquer. Let's stop judging others by their methods of bringing people to know Jesus. For example: Kirk Franklin and God's Property with their smash hit "STOMP!" Many people were complaining and saying things such as, "That is Satan in that song or in that group!" In my mind and heart, Kirk Franklin has done a great thing. You might ask how. Well, he found a way to reach our youth when the world had given up on them (calling them the Generation X group). The world says that this new generation has no guidelines, morals, rules and most of all, direction. If so, as Christians, it is our obligation to see that our youth are not lost to Satan. In this chapter, you will find that I have summaries with a few of my poems to give you, the reader, a better understanding of what I am trying to say. As you read, I pray that one will touch or encourage you to go out and spread God's love to someone. God's love deserves to be shared and multiplied. Together, let's plant God's seed, making His love multiply!

A Silent Cry

Every night, I begin to cry;
For it's about to start and
I don't know why...
I want to be strong and take a stand;
But how, when he's using his hands...
See, my mind is saying, "Fight!"
But my body is saying,
"No more bruises tonight..."
What must be done to over come
this obstacle which is in my way?
I'm so all alone, really afraid to leave home...
Someone please hear my cry;
Help me before it's too late. Help me before I die...
I'm tired of being abused; Yet, I'm scared
and also confused.
Heavenly Father, please give me strength.

A Right That's Mine

I hide behind this mask,
so that you won't have to ask,
of why I cry...
See, there is a feeling here,
somewhat unclear,
you say it's love, I say it's fear...
Pain is the only thing in store and
I'm not gonna take it anymore...
This so-called thing you call love,
you know, the abuse that you give
to me behind closed doors...
I'll stand my ground, meaning no more
abusive nights; For I am a woman
with many rights and I have the
right, to choose not to fight...

Enough

I have been through so much;
Trying to cope with all the pain,
mentally from his touch…
Over and over again,
I've wondered why? Enough!
This madness must come to an end;
I'm fed up with being a victim, no
longer will I pretend…
I am going to be firm and stand
proud and tall; If he wants
to continue his abuse,
I'll just make that 911 call…
Remember,
no one deserves abuse!

A Silent Cry, A Right That's Mine & Enough Summary:

Women who were actually being abused inspired me to write these three poems. Coming from a Christian man, I am trying to encourage men all across the world to be good Godly men. Meaning that we need to take a stand and treat our women with admiration, love and respect. We also need to encourage other brothers who DO abuse their mates, to make a change.

We must remind them that women are a part of God. We are to love them, not batter them. See, in 1 Corinthians 13:4-5,7 we are told that, "Love is patient and that love is kind." "It's not rude, nor easily angered, it keeps no record of wrongs…" "It always protects, always trusts, always hopes, always perseveres." Also, in Ephesians 5:28 it says, "Husbands ought to love their wives as their own bodies. He who loves his wife loves himself." Now, think about that for a second, if you are battering your wife, then you may as well be beating yourself also, for your wife is a part of you.

If you find yourself battering your wife, stop! Ask God to forgive you and to change you from this type of behavior. If you feel you are too deep and can not stop on your own, seek assistance either from a friend, counselor, or a pastor. May God bless you!

My Savior Is He

God,
my Savior is He;
Always and forever,
giving me love more
abundantly.
God is the reason we are here;
Full of blessings
and lots of cheer.
Give Him the praise that He is
entitled to;
And let Him continue
to live inside of you.

My Savior Is He Summary:

In Jeremiah 9:23-24 it says, "This is what the Lord says: "Let not the wise man boast of his wisdom or the strong man boast of his strength or the rich boast of his riches, but let him who boasts boast about this: that he understands and knows me…" It's a wonderful and joyous feeling to know Christ, this is why I wrote the poem *My Savior Is He*. No matter what you do or where you are, let the world know that you love the Lord at all times. "And that His praises shall always be in your mouth,"

Never Too Old

You know,
you're never too old
to express your love and
gratitude, especially to the
foundation of your upbringing.
That's why I want to say,
"Thanks and I love you dad!"
I'll never forget the talks
and the times when you were there
for me. Never having any doubt,
still believing in me...
No one on this earth can change
the way I feel about you and that's
a fact... I love you dad!

Never Too Old Summary:

You know, no matter what I did, my father was always there for me. Even times when I felt that he should have scorned me, he turned to me saying, "I'm not going to tell you what you did wrong because you already know." I thought about what my dad was saying and I came to the conclusion that if you are doing wrong, God will eventually bring it to the light!

My dad is a business man, yet most of all a family man. He taught me how to take control of life by having God first, rather than let Satan and the world take control of me. My dad (Michael L. Johnson) is the best and I love him with all my heart. Remember, the Bible says, "Honor thy father..."-Exodus 20:12.

Mother, I Need...

Every night,
it's the same old thing;
It seems that disappointment
to you, I only bring...
Mother,
I never meant to cause
you any pain; I only wanted
to be closer to you,
your heart I wanted to gain...
I'd do any and everything
just to try and please you;
Hoping that you would
remember, that I am an
extension of you...
Mother, I need your loving!

Mother I Need...Summary:

Throughout my high school days, I thought I was all alone. Not sure of who I was or where I was going, until I met people who didn't have both parents like I had. I can recall a friend that stayed only with his mother, who got away with everything. His mother let him roam the streets, stay out as late as he wanted and if he was to get in trouble in school, she would only say, "If you are going to do something, don't get caught doing it because I don't have time to come up to your school!" To other kids, this was cool, but in reality, it wasn't.

By his mom not teaching him morals and disciplining him, his life was headed in the wrong direction. As he got older, he kept finding himself in trouble with the law, looking to his mom to save him. At the age of 25, he is still trying to find himself. He blames his mother for the way that he is. See, in Proverbs 13:24 we are told, "He who spares the rod hates his son, but he who loves him is careful to discipline him." My friend's mother let him get away with so much for so long, that all he knows is what is wrong. Parents, we must teach our children about God. As spoken in Proverbs 23:14, we are to "train up a child in the way he should go, and when he is old he will not turn from it." I have three boys and I pray everyday that God will give me the insight to keep them on the path of righteousness. I know that I must be their example and not let the world be their example. Mothers, love your children and please discipline your children!

A Blessing

Over-turned in the south bound lane,
shocked and confused,
feeling somewhat deranged...
With a swollen face,
I look to my right,
come to find that my child
is nowhere in sight...
I look in the back seat to see
if my child is there,
no luck, oh Lord where...?
Suddenly a voice shouts from
the front of the car,
"She's up about five yards!"
Could it be my child that is
laying in the street,
Oh Lord, I forgot to buckle
my child's seat...
Even though I was careless,
God had given me another try;
My child only suffered minor injuries,
it's a blessing that my child didn't die...
PLEASE BUCKLE UP!

A Blessing Summary:

    Sometimes we get so caught up in the way that the world is living, we lose sight of how we are supposed to be living. That is, living Christ-like. We get in the mode of, if I do this which is wrong, I'll just ask God to forgive me afterwards. This isn't being a faithful servant to God. This isn't being Christ-like. See, in Matthew 19:17 it says, "If you want to enter life, obey the commandments." What if God had not died on the cross for you and me and had said, "They are not worth me sacrificing my life."? Do you think that you would be here now? Good question huh?

    The poem *A Blessing* shows you how one minute you are alive and how the next minute you could be dead. Don't take life for granted!

Hear His Words...

I hear words from the chaplain
flow as I lay in my bed;
Drifting in and out of consciousness,
I hear a whisper, "Is he dead?"
Lord, give me strength,
Father, I now repent,
for the things in which I have done;
Is it to late? Wait! Wait!
I'm only 18, my life has just begun...
My life, flashing before me;
Oh Lord, please have mercy...
I cry for another chance as the light begins to fade;
I now know that death can come at anytime,
as well as any age...
My mind begins to spin, my heart rate descends,
Is this the end?
Awakened by a beep,
the good Lord saved me,
my soul He now keeps...
Hear His Words!

Hear His Words Summary:

    Today in life, we are faced with gangs and it seems like they are on the rise. Every time I look in the newspaper, it seems that another youth has lost his life due to gang affiliation. What is so fascinating about being in a gang? Yes, there are a lot of people in with you, but they can never take the place of family. Most of all, they can never take the place of God. The love that God has waiting for you is gentle, soft, heartfelt and most of all, warm. He puts a feeling of serenity around you. He can also give you peace.

    All you have to do is repent for your sins and accept Christ into your heart. Acknowledge that Jesus is your Savior and that you no longer live for yourself, but for Him. Whatever you do, hear his words! Remember what Matthew 10:22 says, "He who stands firm to the end will be saved!"

Labeled A Failure

Labeled a failure by my own kind;
Put down in every way
because I'm not afraid to use my mind…
Accused, tried, and judged
for wanting to live for Christ completely;
That's all right,
for God,
I'll serve a dozen life sentences,
proud and faithfully…
No matter how the world labels me;
I know in my heart that God has something
planned for me…
So, label me what you want
and what you please;
A winner I am,
this is what I will always believe!

Labeled A Failure Summary:

One thing that I have come to know and learn is that whatever you want to do or be in life, go after that dream. No matter what others think or say, remember that God is with you and with God, you cannot go wrong. Just think if I had not accepted Christ because people (who I thought were my friends) were making fun of me and even talking about me behind my back. My soul would have belonged to Satan. Whooo! I wouldn't even give Satan the satisfaction, so don't you give those that label you a failure that satisfaction either!

If you put God first in all that you do, it doesn't matter what anyone may think or say, God will see you through. Always remember this verse: "You will do great things and surely triumph."- 1 Samuel 26:25 (NIV).

Standing Firm

Standing with the Lord is
where we should all be;
Focusing on the richness of His word,
not sinful fantasies…
Standing tall we should always do;
Even when trials and tribulations
seem to find you…
Remember, God gave us
eternal encouragement and hope!

Standing Firm Summary:

What would life be like if we didn't have faith in God? We'd probably be lost in sin forever. There are some people in the world who actually do not stand firm in their faith. Meaning that one must commit to the teachings of God at all times, even in trying times. One must have faith to know that God will never forsake us. If there is no faith, then you are basically, already Satan's.

See, in Isaiah 7:9 it says, "If you do not stand in your faith, you will not stand at all." We can't let Satan win. We owe it to Christ to go out and spread His word. No matter what you may face, stand firm in your faith!

Case Closed

Locked down for a crime
that I didn't commit;
Accused of murder,
I never thought it would stick...
The system took me in,
processed and booked;
Never once did it wonder,
nor take a second look...
At the fact that I've
always taken the honest road;
All that seem to matter is
"Case closed!"

Case Closed Summary:

Throughout life, we are falsely accused of either doing or saying something. I can recall a time in my life when I told the truth, but yet I was still accused of doing wrong. No matter what anyone believed, I knew that I was innocent and that God would let the truth soon be known. Even through all the turmoil I still continued to have faith in God. If you refer back to Psalms 55:12 we are told to "cast your cares on the Lord and He will sustain you; He will never let the righteous fall!" This is what I believed and you know what, the truth finally surfaced. Case closed! Whatever you do, KEEP THE FAITH!

On My Knees

Father, I know that I have not
done of what you have asked of me;
I'm coming to you now,
giving you my life completely…
Giving you thanks for everything
that you have done; There is no greater
love than you, you're the Holy One…
So, on my knee's, I pray to you;
That I'll put you first in all that I do…
My life has completely changed;
I love you Jesus and I'm glad
I can call your name…
And I know that you are watching
over me; Lord, I'm here to do your will.
I can't sit still.
I live for you completely!

On My Knees Summary:

    A few years ago, I used to be a busy R&B music producer. Touring with different local and national recording artists just thinking that I was on top of the world. In reality, I was at the bottom and getting deeper. I became caught up in myself, the money, and all of the attention, forgetting about who I really should have been focusing on and that was Jesus.

    Jesus was the one who gave me this talent and I must use it to glorify Him and not myself. So, I, from this day forth it shall be all about living completely for Him and I am not ashamed to get down on my knees for Him!

    Remember what Matthew 5:16 says, "In the same way, let your light shine before men, that they may see your good deeds and praise your Father in Heaven."

Sing Out Loud

For many years, you find yourself being what the world wants you to be; Living in so much sin, afraid to face reality... But somehow, your life flashes before your very own eyes; Blinding you, leaving you to only hear sad and lonely cries... But then Jesus reaches down and pulls you from the crowd; He says, "Your work is not yet done, go and sing out loud!" Go and tell the world about His love; Let the world know that Jesus is the one you're always thinking of... With Jesus on your mind and in your heart, you can't help, but to carry on; Put Him above all things that you do, with Jesus you can't go wrong... He's a feeling that can't be labeled; Give Him your all and for Him, you should always be willing and able...
Go sing out loud!

Sing Out Loud Summary:

What good is it for one to have a talent and not use it for God? It is only good for pleasing one's own self. See, we should use our gifts to promote Jesus Christ and His word. If we put Jesus in all that we do and say, the blessings will no doubt be far greater than what the world would try and offer you. The world can only give you materialistic items, not salvation.

We are given these talents to bring others to know Christ. For me, I accept my calling which is to write Christian poetry that will educate others about the word of God all across the world. I must be honest with you, I wasted a lot of years trying to please myself, but now I have been found. I am on a mission for God and that's to sing out loud how He has changed me and my life forever. I can definitely say that I have a personal relationship with God by how much time I spend talking to Him, by how much I try and be like Him, most of all, by how I want Him to use me for His needs.

See, in I Corinthians 6:19-20 we are told that, "You are not your own, you have been bought with a price." This means that God owns you completely and He wants to use you daily for His will. Love Him as He loves you. Always sing out loud how He has touched and changed your life. Without Him, there would be no you or me! Let the world know what He has done!

Trust In Me

I know that you have things
that are on your mind;
Just give it to Jesus, He'll
heal all wounds in time...
I'm here for you whenever
you might be down;
So look to me for support,
I'll always be around...
Trust in me to be your friend;
Trust in me through thick and thin.

Trust In Me Summary:

Don't let life get the best of you. You must remember that God will not give you more than you can bare. He is always right there for you. Assuring you that He will not forsake you. Just put all of your trust into Jesus and let Him perform His miracles.

I can recall when I had my first major surgery, matter of fact, first surgery ever in my life. I was just plain scared! I guess because I was really insecure in my walk with God to trust in Him completely. As the time came to have the surgery, I could only remember one thing, this operation must take place in order for me to have a normal life. As I laid down on the table, my pastor came in to comfort me, he said, "Son, God is with you!" I just smiled with joy, yet still nervous. Next thing I know, the nurse comes to me saying are you ready? I ask is that a trick question. She began to stick a needle down into my arm, the next thing I know, I'm waking up seeing this bright light and hearing this loud beeping sound. I shouted aloud, "Where am I?" The nurse said, "You are in the recovery room!" Man, I couldn't believe that the surgery was over that fast. I never knew that I was out or better yet, alive.

After going through this surgery, I learned to trust in God completely, rather than partially. Also, my faith in God is where it should have been in the very beginning, at the highest point. God is so good to us and we sometimes take His grace and love for granted. Well, for me, no more! My life is dedicated to serving the Father forever!

Remember, "Cast thy burden upon the Lord and He shall sustain thee: He shall never suffer the righteous to be moved." -Psalm 55:12

The Visit

Whispers, I hear in the night;
My heart pounding with fear, for
I know that I am not living right...
Walking in the shadows of death,
I turn around to confront my fear;
I see a table with a body on it, my mind
wonders, who might it be as I grow near...
I reach for the body, only to hear a voice
crying, "How could this be?" Come to find
that on the table, it was me... The visit I had
always feared was here at last; I was all alone,
alone to review my past... "Is that me?" I cried aloud.
How could I have been so foolish? I had only accepted
Jesus with my lips and not with my heart. Don't wait
until that visit to accept Jesus with your heart.
For then, it might just might be too late!

The Visit Summary:

Have you ever been in a situation where you met someone and within the next few weeks that person died? Well, for me, I have experienced this numerous times. I remember a time when a friend of mine had moved here to Dallas from Lawton, Oklahoma. She was a very intelligent person, just eager to be in love. She concentrated so much on being with this one guy, rather than being with her first love, Jesus. She pursued the gentleman and finally they became a couple. She moved into his apartment. I advised her that she was making a mistake and that God doesn't like for us to do it this way. Meaning, woman and man living together without being married! She just said, "You only go around once!"

Well, a week had passed and as we met up at the studio to do some recording, she said, "Charles, I think I made a mistake!" And I just listened. She went on to say that she thinks her boyfriend has another woman. I then told her, "You need to do the right thing and that is to move out and get your own place." She did agree. Later that night, she seemed to be doing fine.

The next day around noon, I had received a phone call that my friend had shot herself in the eye. My heart just dropped. I couldn't believe that this was happening because she and I had just talked last night. Quickly rushing to the hospital, I called my wife on the car phone, notifying her of what had taken place. She too was in disbelief. On arriving at the hospital, my friend was being rushed to emergency. I got a small glimpse of her face, one side half gone and the other side covered in blood. I ask my other friends, "Why? What happened?" They could all see that I was really shook up by this ordeal. All I could think about was just talking to her on the phone the night before. Whoa!

The doctor came out later to inform us that my friend had died. This was my first time ever really knowing someone who had just died. My life was to never be the same. I finally found out that she committed suicide because of her failing relationship with her boyfriend. You know, life is hard at times, but not so hard that we cannot handle it. My friend died tragically. My point in sharing this with you is to let you know that life is too short to be living without God. You never know when it is going to be your time. Stop taking His love and grace for granted. Find Jesus today. Accept Him with your heart and not just with your mouth! "For the wages of sin is death, but the gift of God is eternal life through Jesus Christ our Lord!" -Romans 6:23. Rest In Peace Twelve!

Give Me A Man's Love

There's a little girl inside of me and she
is all alone; Looking to find security
from the man at home…
But since you are never there;
For love, I'll search elsewhere…
Don't you know, when you are away;
I feel that I have no guidance to make
it through the day…
Give me a man's love the way it is
supposed to be; Teach me to stay pure,
with pride and dignity…
Fathers, teach your daughters
to be Christian women.
Don't let the world teach them
how to be women.

All Is Well With Jesus

Sometimes we have questions.
Questions where the answer only
lies within our Master's plan;
We must continue in faith,
holding on to Jesus' hand…
We know that all isn't easy,
but we know that all will be well,
especially, when it is with Jesus.
My friend,
I lift you and your family
up in my prayers.
God Bless!

I Didn't Want You To Go

I remember seeing you just yesterday;
Full of life, joy, and laughter, no matter
what came your way...
I didn't want to believe that you were no
longer around; See, I kept my head up high,
never once looking down...
Never looking down to face all the pain;
From crying I'm trying to refrain...
For I didn't want you to go. Like a mother
with her child, you watched me grow;
Always showing love to me, wherever
you might go...
With you around, I would always feel
secure and trouble free; For a best friend,
I'd always have within thee...
Thank you for being near, bringing
sunshine all throughout the year...
"Rest In Peace!"

Natural High

God,
my Heavenly Father,
I sometimes just sit and cry;
For I realize what you have given
and what you have done,
so I kneel to one knee, lifting
my hands up high...
Your undying love has
touched me in a special way;
I vow to be an example.
I vow to represent you
everyday...
Lord, I tell you know lie;
Lord, you give to me
a natural high...

No Longer

In a cage for the last 20 years,
tried unjustly
by the ones we're under,
our so-called peers...
It's a disgrace
to see how the system is taking
a liking to our Black race...
Putting us in chains,
our lives being rearranged,
wealth rarely being obtained
by my taken advantage of people...
See, for so long
we have been kept in the dark,
misguided about our heritage,
when will the truth start...
Tied down, we will be no longer,
we must reveal the truth,
for it will make us stronger...
Trusting in God
is the key to change,
No longer will we be taken advantage of,
no longer will we be the same...

See You Soon

Touch and go, some would find this to be
somewhat unfair; But who said, "If you were
not in sight, that your heart was not there?"
A tear I shed, for I must leave you once again;
Don't think that I no longer love you. I'll
always be there, you just say when...
Like the sun, I'll come around; I'll never
forget this love that I have found...
You are a very special part of me;
You took me in with love, making
me a part of the family...
As hard as it is to say good-bye; I will
leave you with a part of my heart,
a poetic letter saying,
"See you soon ...", rather than
a sad good-bye!

Moods
Of
Life